WOODEN TOPS

A Guide to Carving Walking Sticks

Roy Griffin M.B.E.

Dove Valley

My book is dedicated to my family and friends who appreciate my love for carving wildlife and creating walking sticks.

My thanks to those friends and my family for putting up with me while compiling my manuscript. To test everything and make certain it works satisfactorily takes a lot of time so I would like to thank John Roberts and Brandon Brandon for their expert advice.

All artwork and line drawings are by the author.
Photography of finished walking sticks by
John Roberts of Uttoxeter

ISBN 0 9528382 0 6
13-digit ISBN 978-0-9528382-0-3

47 Leighton Road,
Uttoxeter, ST14 8BL

CONTENTS

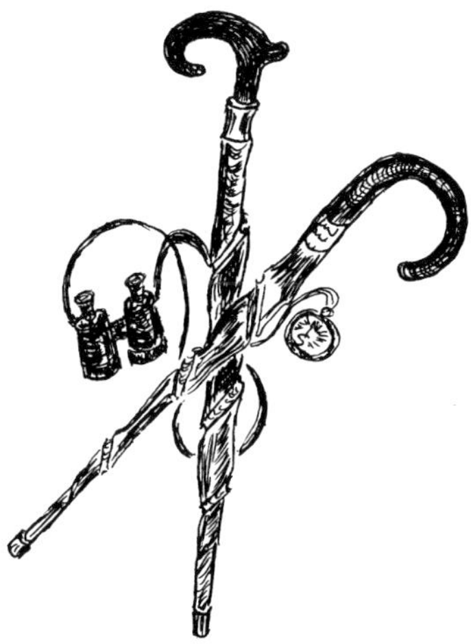

Twisty Sporting Sticks

INTRODUCTION

Whether it to be the need to use a walking stick as an aid for sport or pleasure they have been made for generations.

As an enthusiastic walker walking the banks of the River Dove, one of my favourite haunts for bird spotting, I became interested in carving unusual and creative walking sticks combining the skills of naturalist, artist and wood-carver. Walking sticks can be of a traditional design, or depict wildlife, offering a wide scope for creativity.

All techniques used in the book are tried and tested ones which I have used for many years. The book follows a logical sequence taking the reader through the stages from choice of wood used to make shanks or carving blanks, tools, wood carving, texturing, colouring and finishing. In addition I have included walking sticks made from both horn and antler. Finally a chapter on whistles, shoehorns and buttons made from the off-cuts.

After reading my book you will, I hope, benefit from my experience and produce attractive and satisfying sticks.

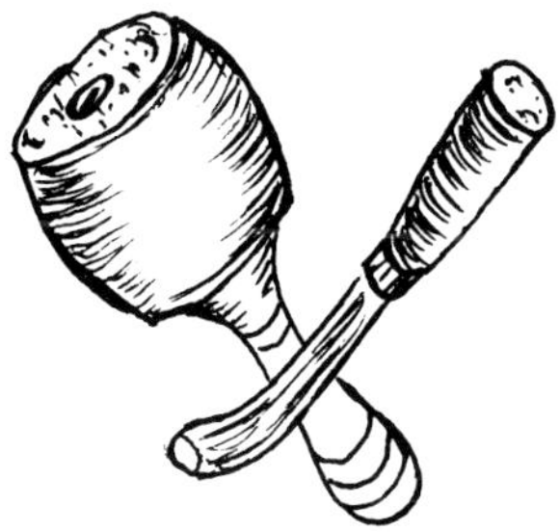

Woodcarving Tools

Chapter 1

TOOLS & ACCESSORIES

One of the attractions of stick carving is that it can be carried out with as many or as few tools as you like starting with just a knife - a stick dresser is never without a pocket or craft knife. Scalpels of surgical steel blades, sold under many names in model and art shops, are a very useful addition for intricate carving. It is best to build up a selection of specialist tools as they are required.

Wood Carving Tools

There is a huge variety of wood-carving tools which, very briefly, can be split up as follows.

Gouges range from a shallow curve to a deep "U" across the cutting edge.

Veiners are deep narrow gouges.

Parting tools, sometimes referred to as a "V" tool, are useful when carving feather or hair texturing.

Skew chisels are a straight chisel with an angled cutting edge.

Curved or bent tools whilst have the same cutting edge as straight ones are curved or bent along the blades length.

Rifflers, Rasps and Files are designed for roughing out and shaping wood, horn etc.

Saws. My tapered Bushman and folding pruning saws are mainly used for cutting sticks, whilst bow, coping and fret-saws are used for fine cutting. Secateurs can be useful for cleaning up raw wood.

Sharpening Tools.

All tools need to be sharpened, slip stones to suit carving gouges etc. flat stones for chisels and knives. It should not be necessary to hone tools each time before carving, so keep a keen cutting edge by polishing on a leather strop charged with a block of crocus powder.

Abrasives

For sanding and finishing come in grades from coarse to fine, steel wool. Grades are 0 grade coarse to 0000 grade fine.

Adhesives

Epoxy resin is a two part adhesive most useful for jointing handles to walking stick shanks, caps and tips on antler in fact most components including ferrules and collars.

Resin "W" is an excellent wood glue, and can also be used as a sealant when diluted with water.

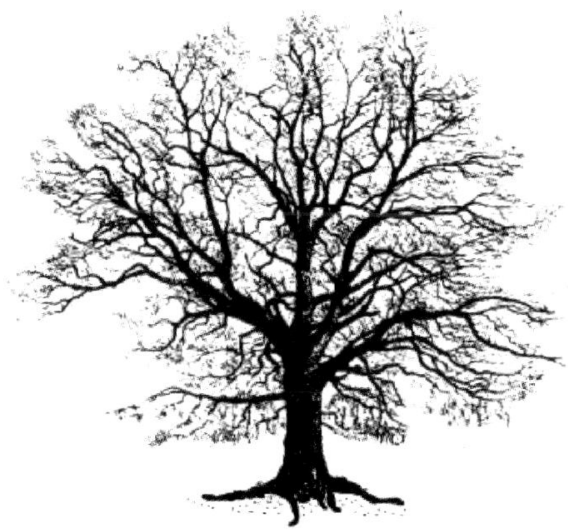

Oak (Quercus Robur)

Chapter 2

TREES, THEIR WOOD & USES

Probably the most used wood by stick dressers is hazel - common hazel (corylus avellana) especially renowned for making one piece crooks, as used in many country crafts. The following, and many others, can be used for making the shanks.

Fruit Woods, most of them are suitable for making walking sticks - but I must mention the Blackthorn (Prunus Spinosa) which makes a most attractive but strong knobbly walking stick, (fruit from Blackthorn are used in the making of Sloe Gin).

Chestnut (sweet) (Castanea Sativa), bent handled National Health walking sticks are made from this wood.

Rowan (Sorbus Aucuparia) (Mountain Ash), a traditional wood for making Shepherd Crooks (the berries have high content in Vitamin C.

Wild Rose (Dog Rose) (Rosa Canina)

Sycamore (Acer Pseudoplatanus)

Holly (Ilex Aquifolium)

Oak (Quercus Robur)

Suitable hardwoods for carving the handles include:

Beech (C) (Fagus Sylvatica)

Elm (English) (Ulmus Procera)

Walnut (Juglans Regia)

Oak (Quercus Robur)

Sycamore (Acer Pseudoplatanas)

A much desired hard wood by Carvers is Burr i.e. Burr Elm because of its most attractive figuration. All Burr woods are regarded as rare and exotic. Bull Banksia (Banksia Grandis) known to us as Banksia Nuts, can be used to turn knob stick handles, and Laburnum (Common) (Laburnum Anagyroides) which is used for decorative carving and in musical instruments.

Softer woods for carving and ideal for a beginner are Lime (Tilia Sp) and Ivy (Hedera Helix) then comes Hazel (Common Hazel).

A stick with a block on top is commonly called a Block Stick. Many varied designs or creative walking sticks can be carved from these including Shepherds Crooks.

Chapter 3

SHANKS

Cutting

It is prudent to obtain permission from the Landowner to walk his land to cut sticks. Sticks should be cut between December and February when the sap is low, cutting outside this period should be avoided as difficulties in seasoning occur because the amount of sap in a freshly cut stick needs extra care when drying out. A stick needs to be cut "longer" than required if possible, and the thickness depends upon the type of stick being made. When stick cutting be careful, wear thornproof clothing and eye protection.

Seasoning

After a stick cutting session, I check my assortment and prepare them for seasoning, they are tied in convenient sized bundles and are labelled with the date and place of origin.

A golden rule is never to speed up the drying out of the sap and do not bring the stick indoors too soon. During the seasoning period the bark should be left on, however some sticks may suffer from the bark becoming flaky and start to peel off. Always leave the thorns on a dog rose until after seasoning. Some woods are harder than others and these need extra care when drying out.

A guide for seasoning can be based on one year for every inch of diameter. I normally take precautions when seasoning sticks, of coating the end grain with a little paraffin wax. Those sticks which are prone to bark wrinkling or flaking during seasoning can be cleaned with white spirit and given an application of a coat of varnish - this should be done within a few days of cutting, I always treat Holly in this way.

Straightening Shanks

Before straightening a shank, trim off any unwanted pieces, twigs, thorns etc.

Steam heat or dry heat. Steam is very dangerous and every precaution should be taken in choosing this type of apparatus. Steaming times vary with the type of wood and thickness of the shank, trial and error will perfect the correct timings. When applying heat in this way several shanks can be steamed.

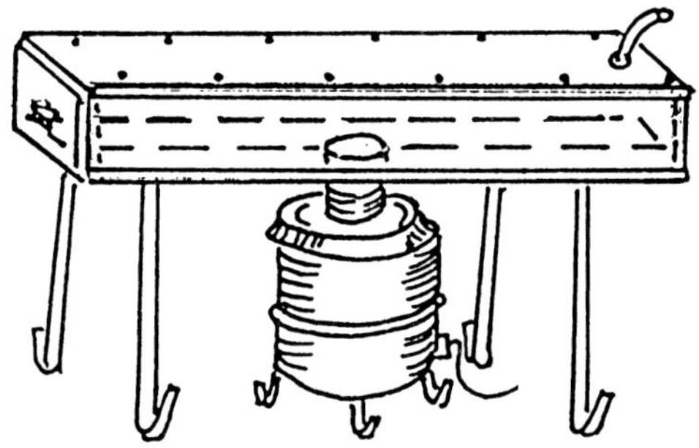

Fig 1 *Steamer made from marine grade plywood 12mm thick. The inside measures 150mm x 130mm (6"x 5"). Cut a hole in the base to connect the boiler and rack inside to hold the sticks on. The legs can be fitted to slope the bottom so the condensation can run away. For safety fit a steam outlet.*

Dry Heat

Can be applied by placing the shanks on top of a double radiator, the wood does not take long to warm up. Alternatively a hot air gun can be used, providing that the gun is kept moving so as not to damage the bark, should the bark get damaged there is no way it can be turned back to its natural state. Apply heat along the shank, thicker parts may need to be heated longer. Cutting corners by using excessive heat will only damage the bark.

The fibres of the wood need to be heated gradually, whichever method is used once the shank is pliable it can be straightened. I use a set of leather faced blocks in a vice as a wide variety of positions can be obtained. Locate the offending bent area of the pre-heated shank on the front block, wind up the vice until the shank slightly bows between the two rear blocks. Each area to be straightened can be dealt with by moving the shank's position while it is still warm. If the wood cools down, the process can be repeated if necessary. Finally, the shank can be placed on a cool floor, the fibres will retract and the shank will set in a straight position.

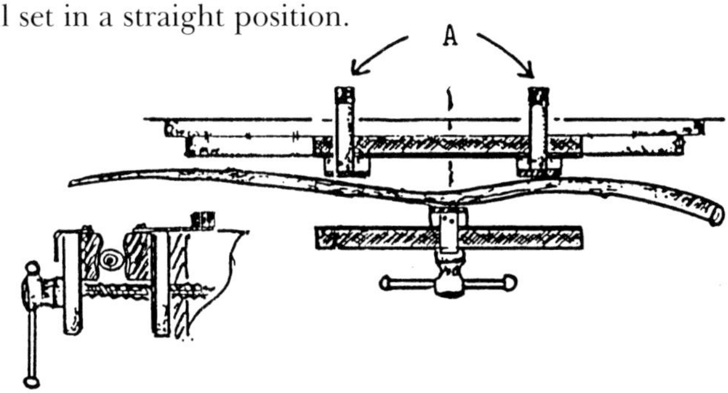

Fig 2 *Straightening blocks, side view. Support the front block on bracket to suit your vice, two rear blocks are fitted with weighted arms = 'A' to steady them when positioning a shank.*

Bark Stripping

Some shanks look better when the bark is stripped off to show the natural grain. If the bark is left on it should be taut and not wrinkled or flaky, otherwise it is best stripped off. The bark can easily be removed by first trimming the outer bark with a sharp knife, should it prove difficult to remove, first soak in warm water and then repeat. The inner bark can be scraped off using the back of a knife blade so as not to damage the wood. The wood can then be rubbed down with abrasive paper or steel wool for a smooth finish.

Sanding Shanks

Before dressing check the shank for any unusual growth, some can be emphasized or a carving created within it. With the bark left on, a light sanding may only be required.

When sanding twisty shanks care must be taken because the twists travel along the stick in no uncertain way simply because during its growing life the tough twisting stem of the Honeysuckle (Lonicera periclymenum), an English woodbine stunts its growth. It has a remarkable way of raising its stem from the soil where the seedling sprouts. It twines spirally clockwise around any woody stem in reach.

I use cloth backed abrasive to dress the inside of the groove where the Honeysuckle has grown, just tear the full length of the sheet into strips about 6mm (¼") wide and use in stropping motion. Abrasive paper can be glued on a flat surface or around a piece of wooden doweling and used in a filing motion.

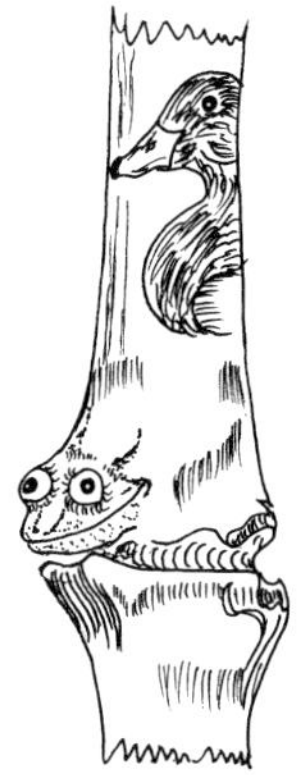

Fig. 3. *Illustration: Wildlife decorated twisty shank enlarged to see detail. Frog created in distorted section.*

Abrasives

An abrasive flexible foam rubber block is Ideal for sanding, as it will shape itself round the shank while being dressed. I normally start with a medium grade on bare wood in all cases try to sand in the direction of the wood grain.

After the first sanding stages revert to fine foam backed sanding pads (these are far thinner than the sanding blocks) and use to the finest grade it takes to get a satisfactory finish. *(Refer to Fig. 3).*

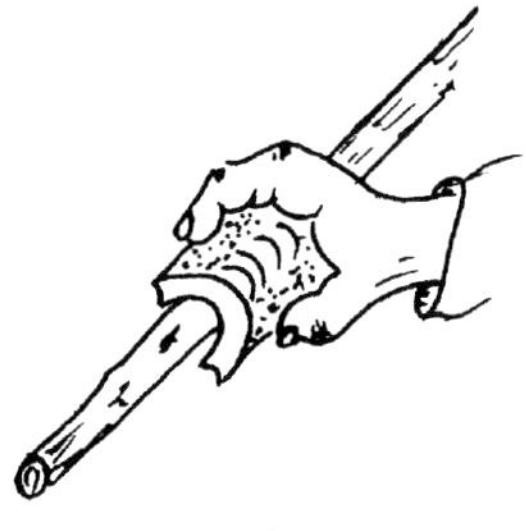

Fig. 3a. *Illustration: Flexible Sanding Block*

Steel wool grades are O grade course to 0000 grade fine, the finest grade is ideal for final finishing and applying a wax polish as it will also burnish the wood.
Drum sanders, are very useful they are normally used in a bench drill, useful for e.g. sanding carved heads crook handles and shanks. If after abrading carving tools are being used always wash the wood with Methylated Spirits to remove any grit.

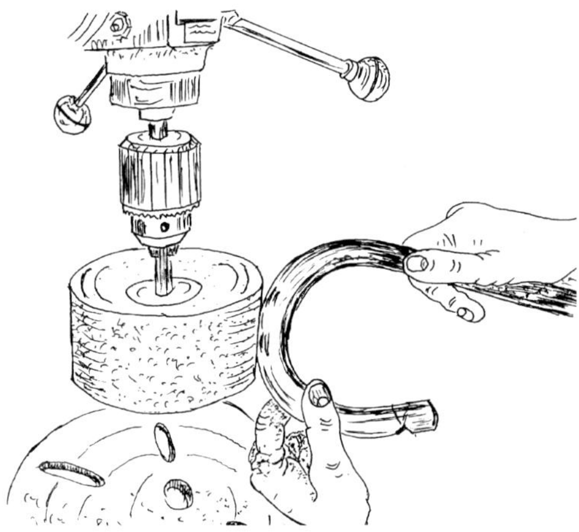

Illustration:
Drum Sander (Sanding the crown on a steam bent handle)

Drum sanders come in sets of various sizes and normally made of rubber, larger ones as illustrated 130mm (5") diameter and made of foam rubber and are more flexible.
When using sanding equipment it is advisable to wear a dust mask and eye protection.

Chapter 4

CARVING

There is a choice of two methods of creating fancy heads.

If a coloured finish is required, where texturing has been used, a close grain wood is best or a natural wood finish. This enables the wood grain to be shown to its best advantage with a clear final finish.

I like to carve ducks, birds and animals, but I don't stop at that the Shepherds Crooks and Knob sticks are just as interesting. Sticks that have the handle jointed to the shank may be referred to as two piece sticks. One method of jointing is to use engineer's threaded rod, the handle is drilled so that the rod is a push fit, a piece can be glued in prior to any carving so that the rod protruding at the bottom of the cut out blank can be used to grip in the vice when carving. All my walking sticks have the same carving and shanking techniques unless I'm carving a one piece stick, otherwise known as a block stick. Although the preparation is slightly different the marking out and carving techniques are the same, the advantage with block sticks is that you don't have to join the handle to the shank.

First, I will deal with the two piece sticks. A wooden blank needs to be cut about 115mm x 90mm x 48mm (4½" x 3½" x 1⅞") for a head carving and 35mm (1⅜") thick - large enough for the handle design for a Shepherds Crook or a Market Stick.

PATTERNS AND MARKING OUT

Ornamental Handles

I like to take photographs of every angle possible, a profile shot will be beneficial when drawing a pattern onto graph paper. This can be transferred onto a carving blank with the aid of carbon paper. You may wish to refer to books for help with your patterns. Once the blank has been marked out, sawing out the head can be done with a coping saw or band saw. Next, mark a centre line around the cut out head, the base of the neck will be the face joint between the handle and the shank, mark the centre and drill a - 8mm (5⁄16") hole for the joint pin. The head features can be marked in next to give the correct eye position. Eyes can either be carved within the head or glass ones fitted. For the latter, drill a 3mm (⅛") pilot hole right through the head, this is to ensure when the eyes are finally fitted they are directly opposite one another. On some heads, mainly animals, the eyes are positioned differently so individual pilot holes will have to be drilled later during carving.

Next mark the head shape including the bill, if carving a ducks head, and cut away the waste wood tapering the neck slightly. Trim off the corners and rough carve with a shallow gouge or rasp, the lower part of the neck needs to be slightly larger than the top of the shank. The finishing carving is done when it is finally jointed.

Whittle the head down to size and make sure the carving looks right working on one proportion at a time, using your photographs for reference, and carve to a mirror image. If carving an animal or a bird like an owl, the pilot holes for the eyes can be drilled about 16mm (⅝") into the head with 3mm (⅛") drill. Carve the head until satisfied with the appearance and enlarge the pilot holes to form the eye sockets (about the depth of the eye to be fitted) When carving a birds bill, especially on a duck, take careful note of its shape as it is an important feature. Some carvers purchase 'study bills' made of plastic for reference. A carved head can be left as a smooth natural finish or textured.

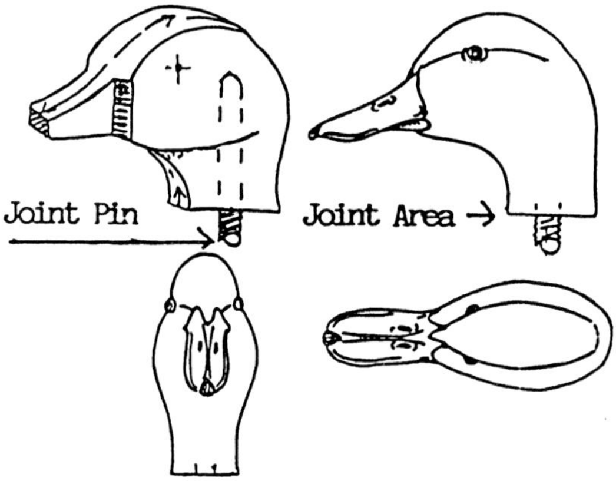

Fig 4 *Head features of Mallard Duck. Centre line marked all round the head, drill 3mm (⅛") pilot hole for the eye position. Third actual size.*

Feather, or hair texturing, can be achieved with a small veiner gouge or "V" parting tool. Start texturing from behind the bill or nose toward the back of the head with short strokes of an irregular pattern, but leave the lower part of the neck. Texturing can also be done by pyrography as described later. (Other head details are shown in figs. 30 & 31).

CROOKS, MARKET AND KNOB STICKS

Crook Sticks.

When marking out in a crook handle shape i.e. in Burr Elm, a transparent template is an advantage, it can be positioned on the blank to see the most effective grain pattern. The grain may run parallel to the handle neck but will alter its direction due to the handle shape. It is important to mark the inside of a crook handle first, the outer mark will follow in accordance with the inner mark. Now cut away the inside of the handle first, so as to make certain sufficient gap has been allowed for, then cut away the unwanted wood on the outer shape.

There is often confusion as to the size a crook handle should be, varieties of sheep differ so should crook handles, a Shepherd would produce a crook to suit his needs.

Fig 5 Crook Handles. Areas and suggested Sizes.
Neck Crook 'A' = 75mm to 90mm (3" - 3½")
Leg Crook 'B' = 32m m (1¼")
'C' = 27mm (1 1/16")
'D' (both) = 12mm (½") = height of nose above joint area
Sizes may differ according to type.

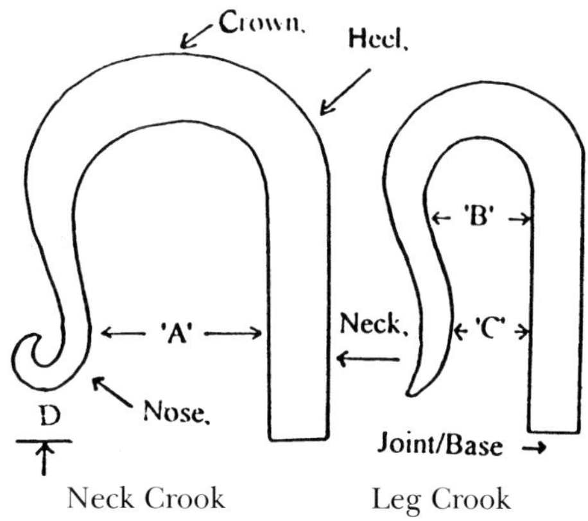

When carving try to carve in the direction of the grain, if against the grain steady the blade with the other hand. Trim off the corners around the handle shape and taper the nose on the crook handle. Carve the handle to your satisfaction and then sand with abrasives to a smooth finish. *(Refer to page 12).*

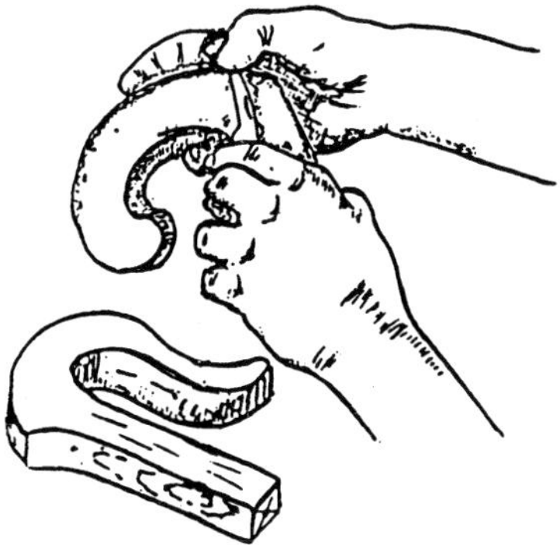

Fig 6 *Top market stick handle. Lower - crook handle blank.*

Knob Sticks

Knob stick handles can be turned or shaped by hand using any hard wood but a Banksia nut when turned makes a comfortable general purpose walking or hiking stick. A compass can also be fitted into the knob if desired. When carving these types of handles the hole for the joint pin can be drilled when most convenient as it depends on the type of handle and how it is made. Joint pins are normally glued into most types of handles first, (before shanking) using epoxy resin adhesive. The glue will squeeze out a little when the pin is pushed into the handle, cramp until set and the glue can be trimmed off when dry. (For fitting a handle to a shank refer to Jointing Methods, Fig. 22).

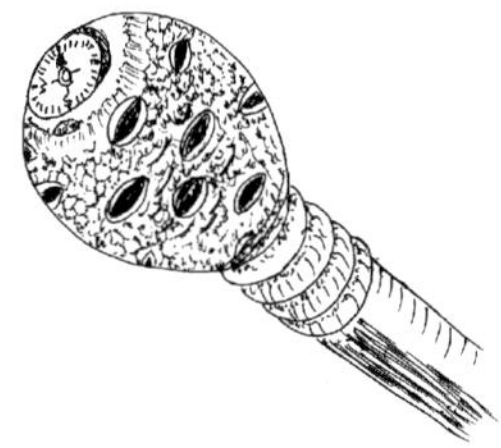

Illustration: Banksia Nut knob stick with built in compass.

When a joint pin is fitted in the knob stick (refer to "A" Fig 22) use a brass one as this should not affect the mechanism of the compass.

ONE PIECE STICKS

Wooden Block Sticks

Hazel is the favoured wood for this type of all wooden stick or crook. The branch intended for the shank sprouts at an angle from the middle of a larger branch, and are suitable to carve as a Shepherds crook or fancy handles. The shank can be straightened the same way as any other shank.

First cut the side cheeks off the block leaving it a rectangular shape about 48mm (1⅞”) thick for a fancy head and 35mm (1⅜”) for a Shepherds crook. Marking out and carving a one piece stick is done the same way as other walking sticks.

Cutting the outside of the handle shape last means it is possible to get the inside shape to the width required. Carve the handle to a rounded shape then finish with cloth backed abrasive with a stropping movement just tear the pieces about 20mm wide (Refer to page12).

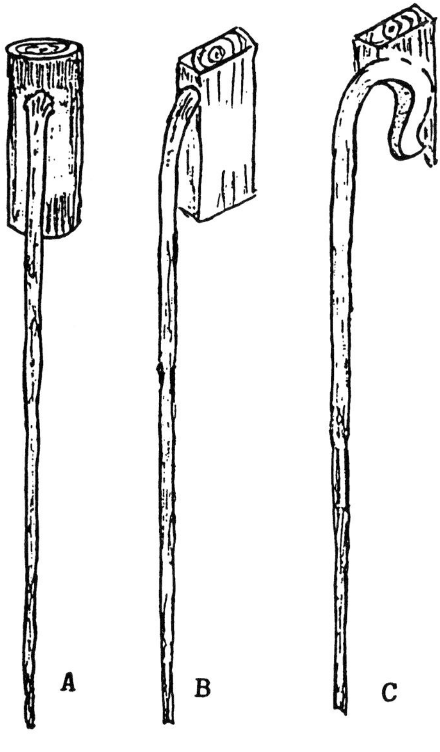

Fig 7 *'A' Block stick blank,*
'B' side cheeks cut off the block,
'C' cut the inside shape of a crook handle first.

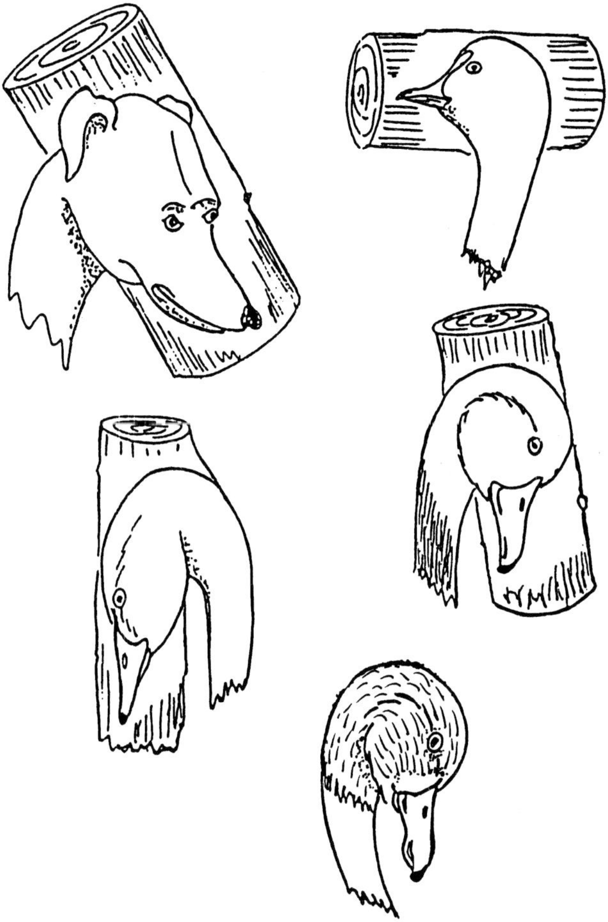

Fig 8 *Block Stick Patterns.*
Top left to right. Lurcher Dog ⅓rd size - Moorhen ⅓rd size Centre left to right. Goose ⅓rd size, Duck suitable for Wigeon or Scaup shape ¼ size. Bottom finished shape. The sizes are approximate as the size of the head will also depend upon the block diameter.

Cross Head and Root Knob Sticks

These are readily formed sticks that have been cut at the root of a shrub below ground level and make an ideal general purpose walking stick, When carving the handle remove as little of the bark as necessary and shape to a smooth, natural finish as shown in Fig.9.

Thumb Sticks

Probably one of the easier sticks to make with its naturally grown fork at the top. When dressing and shaping the fork, care must be taken so that your thumb comfortably fits the fork.

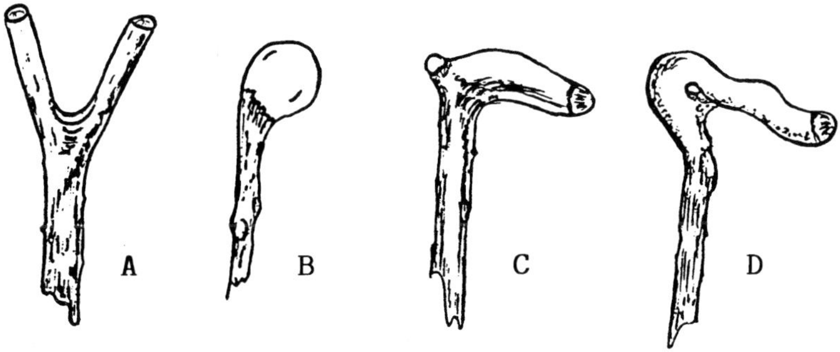

Fig 9 *A = Thumb Stick, B = Root Knob Stick, C & D = Cross Head Sticks.*

Steam Bent Handles

To bend walking sticks, the end to be bent is pushed into hot, damp sand. The simple requirement for this process is a metal tray heaped with damp sand and a heat source underneath. Several shanks can be dealt with at the same time by pushing the top 381mm (15") into the pre-heated sand. The sand will require charging with water at intervals to maintain enough dampness to produce the steam. *(Refer to Fig. 10).*

Only trial and error will perfect the steaming time for a shank to be pliable enough to be formed on a wheeled jig. If the intention is to bend three handles then three jig wheels are required as a stick has to be left on the wheel until the handle is set in position. *(Refer to Fig. 11).*

Preparation for Steaming

The thicker end of the shank will need a notch cutting into it about 25mm (1") from the end and then a piece of string is tied round the notch. The string, when bound and tied to the top of the shank holds it in position on the wheel whilst setting in place after forming. The wheel jig must be secure on a work surface, at the same time ensuring you can get a full swing around the wheel with the length of the shank.

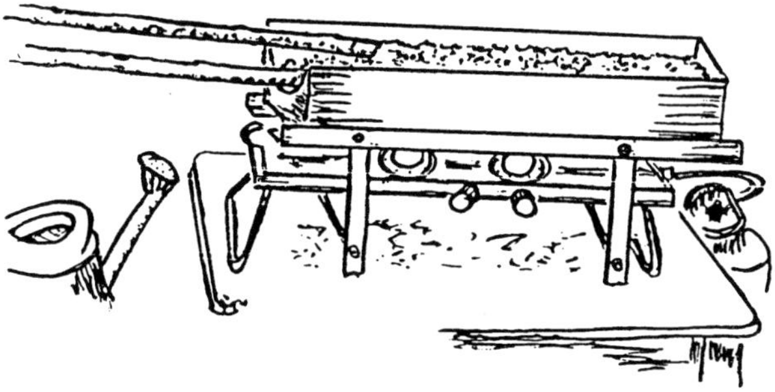

Fig 10 *Steaming Apparatus*

After steaming a shank the handle shape can be formed by placing it on the peg just below the wheel and about 25mm (1") past the notch. Make sure the notch is facing outwards, now swing the shank around the wheel until it nearly touches the end with the string on, and then secure the string around the shank top (the neck of the handle). At this stage some splintering may have occurred at the crown. This is due to insufficient steaming but can be rectified later.

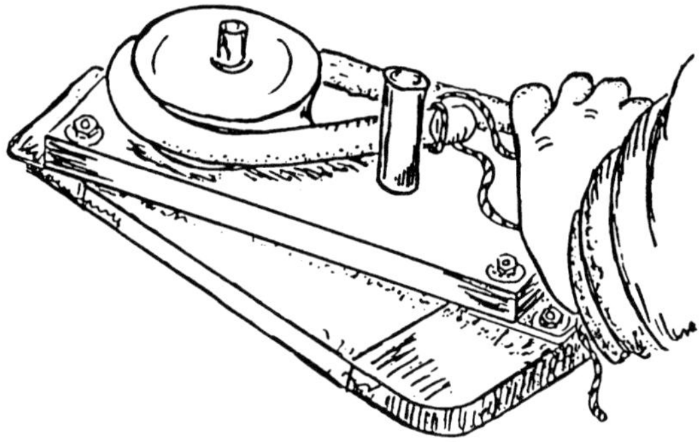

Fig 11 *Forming Wheel Jig for Steam Bent Handles. Dimensions to make wheel jig back plate and wheel in hard wood, wheel size - 120mm (4¾") OD x 50mm (2") wide needs to be free running on a spindle, a lever peg to be located below the wheel, 105mm. (4⅛") centres.*

When the handle has set the string can be cut, it may flex a little making it easier to remove the forming wheel. Now any of the handles that have splintered on the crown can be very carefully removed and the area dressed, sanding to a smooth finish. If a market stick handle is required, cut off above the notch and round off the nose. However, for a crook handle, with the nose turned out, trim to suit and taper this area slightly. Carve the notch and nose to form a crook handle shape. *(Refer to Sanding on page 13).*

Pyrography

Sometimes referred to as wood burning or poker work. Feather or hair texturing can be achieved in a similar way to carving the texture with wood carving tools. Sometimes I combine the two by carving the more pronounced areas and create the rest of the texturing by burning (pyro texture). In some cases it might be necessary to only part texture a head, showing the wood to be the lighter areas of the head. It always helps to draw arrows for feather direction with a pencil. Practice on a spare piece of wood of the same type before starting on a carved head for pyro texture. Texturing is done the same way as carving, by short irregular strokes. Some areas on a head may only need to be shaded, especially on a ducks bill, this can be achieved with the flat of a pyrography point.

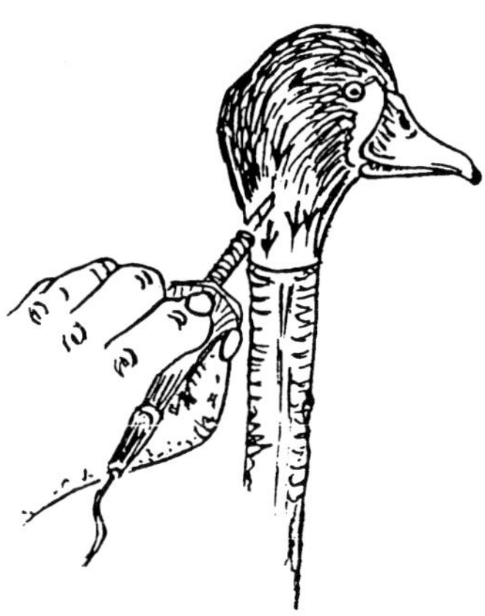

Fig 12 *Finishing, Carving or Pyrography when a handle has been shanked following the arrow direction.*

Chapter 5

GLASS EYES AND HOW TO FIT THEM

Pre-coloured eyes or clear ones can be purchased from Decoy Supplies to the required size. Clear ones need to be painted behind the eye with gloss paint. Most glass eyes are manufactured with a fixing wire and this needs to be cut to suit.

Fitting Eyes

First cheek that the eye sockets are large enough and the right depth, trim if necessary. Eyes can be set in with epoxy adhesive or epoxy putty, both are two part and have to be mixed. It is important to apply the adhesive or putty to the eye socket, work on one eye at a time. Before fitting the eyes trim the wires then, push them through a small ball of epoxy putty already applied to an eye socket. The wire passes down the pilot hole and guides the eye into the socket. Never use anything sharp to adjust the eye, use the rubber end of a pencil as the rubber will not damage it. When pressure is applied to the eye the epoxy putty will squeeze up the sides forming an eye ring or lid. This can be trimmed to suit before the putty dries.

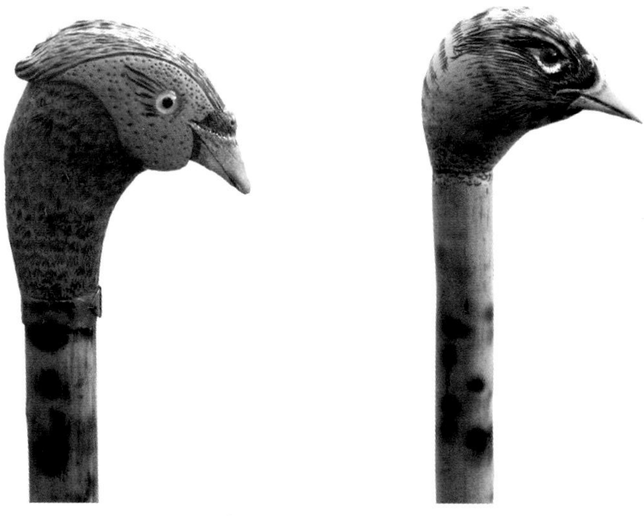

Head detail of natural finish Cock & Hen Pheasants (ornamental sticks) in Elm & Sycamore, both fitted with glass eyes.

Chapter 6

HORN AND ANTLER MATERIALS

The various sorts can be listed as :

Buffalo Horn; ideally suited for stick dressing because it is already partly shaped and is solid.

Cow Horn; careful forming is required as the horn is hollow for most of its length. Also suitable for making shoe horns.

Rams Horn; hollow at the base but easy to work with.

Deer (Family Cervidae); stag antler from Red Deer are widely used by stick dressers. Indian Deer, Chital (axis or spotted deer) and Sambar Deer.

I never discard any horn or antler off cuts because these come in useful when making whistles, buttons and walking stick accessories.

HORN AND ANTLER HANDLES

Shepherds Crooks, Market Stick & a Trout

Before starting with horn you will require a large engineers vice, a woodworkers sash cramp, a steel press large enough for flattening horn, a hot air gun (paint stripper), rasps and files, a set of steel or wooden bulking jigs 50mm (2"), 38mm (1½") and 32mm (1¼"), a selection of hardwood blocks, a half round post and shaped formers.

It is not essential to have elaborate equipment, the jigs I have used for shaping and forming horn are a guide and can be altered to suit your needs.

Horn, like rams horn, will become pliable enough to work after careful penetration of heat.

Heat the entire horn in water, boil gradually and then turn to a lower heat setting, simmering for at least one hour. Horn should only be boiled once as it tends to revert back to its natural state. Some horns don't have to be boiled, all the shaping can be done with the heat from a hot air gun.

Boiling is only recommended for the first stage. Flattening involves moving any curl of the horn level with the base and squeezing in a press. Leave in this position until set. After flattening cut the base off square to the proposed handle neck.

Now the horn may have 50 to 75mm (2" to 3") of hollow at the base. The wall could do with being 8mm (5⁄16") or more, trim off any unwanted horn and rasp to a more uniform shape.

Shaping Using a Hot Air Gun.

Heat a little more than the part being shaped, about 50mm (2") at a time. Apply heat to both sides of the horn so as it penetrates to the centre. Always keep the heat source moving on the horn to prevent scorching.

After heating, the heel being in a pre-formed shape, is the first bend from the angle of the neck to the crown, by trapping a wooden post between the front jaw of the vice and the inside of the horn, a block of wood at the back and squeeze the horn moving the position as required. (refer to Fig. 13) (for areas and sizes refer to Fig. 5)

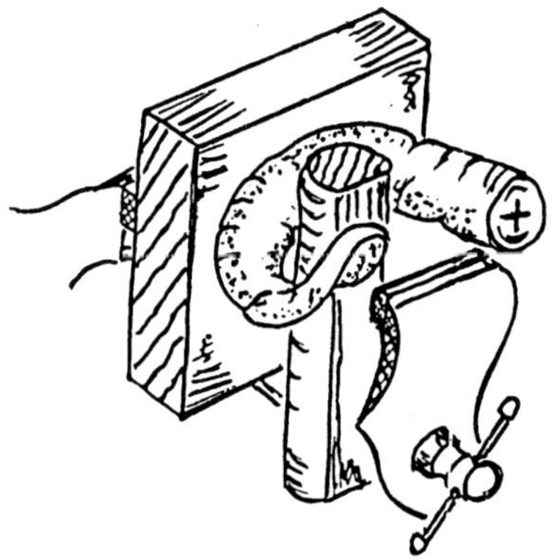

Fig 13 *Shaping Jig. Consists of vice back plate, and a shaped wooden post.*

Bulking up, applying heat along the neck from the heel to the base (hollow end). First use the largest bulking jig the position can be moved to accommodate the part of the horn being squeezed, if the hollow base has started to re-open I push a wooden dowel as far as it will go, this prevents the wall from caving in when bulking, it also tells me the depth of the hollow. Further bulking will be necessary, just repeat the process using a smaller bulking jig. When bulking up the nose to the heel this can be done in the shaping jig (see Fig 13).

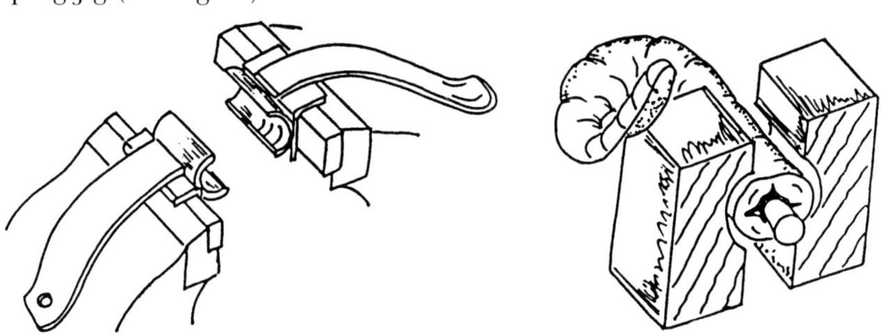

Fig 14 *Bulking Jigs. Left - fabricated from metal, Right - made in hardwood*

Forming

After re-heating, the handle can be shaped by using a sash cramp with a flat jaw to position on the horn and a half-round one to locate on any of the steel pegs. Squeeze up the horn's position as required, re-heating whilst still in the jig if necessary. Leave cramped in it's formed position until set with wedges or segments (refer to Fig. 15).

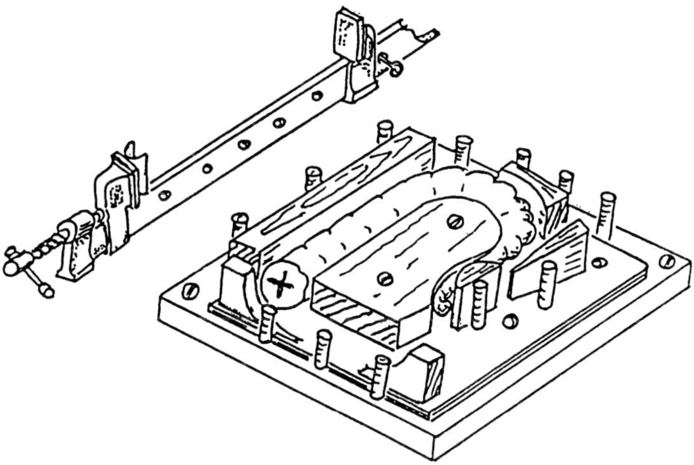

***Fig 15** Horn Forming Jig. This consists of a steel base with a piece of plywood on top. Holes are drilled through, around the wooden former, peg-board style, for 13mm (½") hardened steel pegs.*

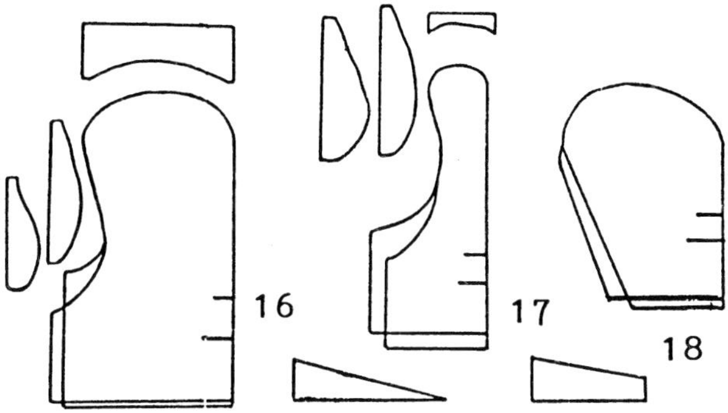

***Figs 16,17,18.** Wooden formers for horn, made from hardwood about 30mm thick, with a selection of segments.*
***Fig 16**, Neck Crook. **Fig 17**, Leg Crook. **Fig 18**, Market Stick.*

After removing from the former finish shaping with a rasp or file. When rasping, any horn handle, only do it for the first stages as it can leave deep cuts which are awkward to remove. Revert to medium-cut files and any final scratches can be removed with a cabinet scraper. When rubbing down horn work through the grades (coarse to fine) of steel wool, washing afterwards with water, ensuring all unwanted marks have been removed. Follow with a rubbing down with a proprietary brand of scouring powder applied with dampened cotton wool. Wash all traces of scouring powder off with water and then a final polish with a metal cleaner, such as Brasso, used in the usual way. After a final cleaning of the handle with methylated spirits it should be finished apart from polishing with a clean duster.

Buffalo Horn Forming Jig

An all steel construction jig for forming Buffalo horn is an alternative to using wooden formers. If fixing to a bench make sure a vertical clamp can be used. The illustrated forming jig fig 18a is suitable for forming shepherds crooks and market stick handles.

Because most buffalo horns are quite flat it makes it easier to mark out the handle shape by drawing a line down the centre from the thick end. Then another line each side to the required thickness along the neck, heel and crown then taper down to the nose. Now cut away the waste horn to leave a square shape.

Fig 18a

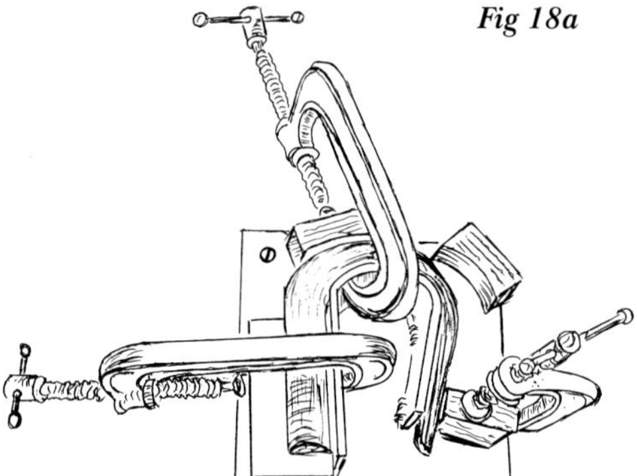

At this stage more horn can be removed if required with a rasp. I prefer to take the corners off and get the horn to a semi round shape before applying any heat. Heat the horn until pliable to bend but keep the horn in a pliable state through the forming process. After heating "G" clamp the neck area to the former, while still pliable make the first bend over the heel and the crown in one move by placing a steel tube (like a scaffold tube) over the nose and secure it with curved hard wood block on the inside of the "G" clamp Fig 18a, all the blocks need to be a sliding fit on the horn, a flat jaw sash cramp can be used in conjunction with the steel tube if required as it will help to pull the horn into the jig shape, then "G" clamp the heel and the crown but the nose will need "G" clamping vertically.

Use as many "G" clamps as required to achieve the handle shape. Leave the clamps in the tightened position until the horn is set.

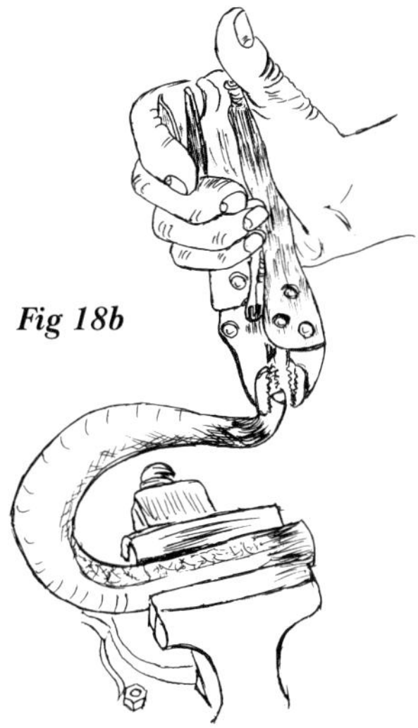

Fig 18b

Forming The Nose

The nose needs to be formed out on a neck crook handle Fig 18b. Re heat the nose very carefully, the nose can be turned out using mole grips, hold the position until cold, it will not take long.

Next stage is explained as already mentioned on page 27. In addition to polishing, Buffalo horn is harder than some and through the stages can buff the horn on a revolving mop, (buffing wheels) this needs to be done when and if required in stages to enhance the natural beauty of the horn.

Polishing compounds can be purchased and used in conjunction with the polishing mops. The mops are manufactured in various sizes to cope with most projects.

Trout, Leaping Pose in Rams Horn

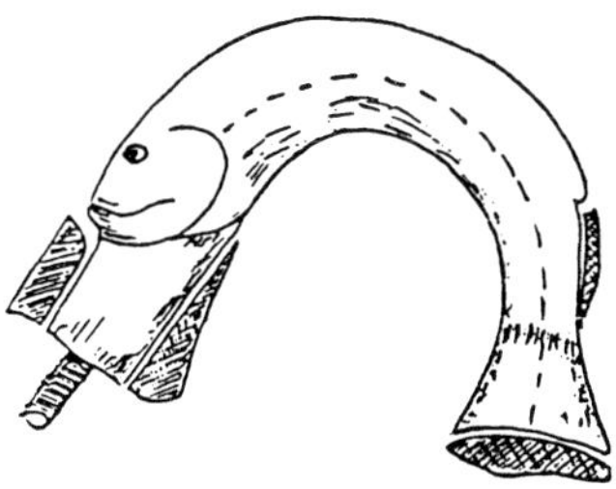

Fig 19 *Cutting out a Trout, the shaded areas are waste horn.*

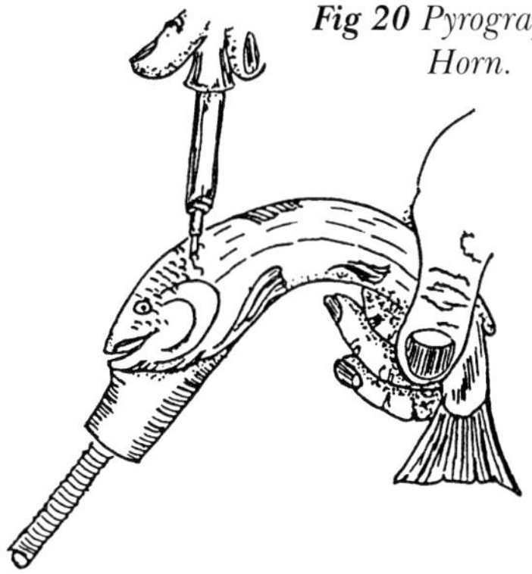

Fig 20 *Pyrography on Horn.*

It is an advantage to obtain a study of a trout for identification purposes when carving and colouring. Because the horn is already part shaped only a little forming will be required. The body may not need a great deal of bulking because a fishes body is oval shaped. The tip of the horn needs to be fairly thick to accommodate flattening for the tail. Any forming or bulking can be done on the shaping jig (Fig. 13).

Mark out the profile, the fishes bottom jaw needs to protract 10mm (⅜") from the handle neck, then cut away any unwanted horn and rasp the body to shape, features can be carved with wood carving tools. Drill a pilot hole through the head for the eye position. I sometimes turn the eyes from Black Buffalo horn and antler and then fashion to suit (see also fitting eyes). Pyro-texture can be achieved when detailing horn, it may get a little charred but can be cleaned with abrasives. *(Refer to pages 12 and 27).*

Fig 21 Finished Trout, after shaping and polishing. Rubbing down and polishing referred to on page 27. The fish can be coloured with drawing inks. Refer to colouring section on page 40.

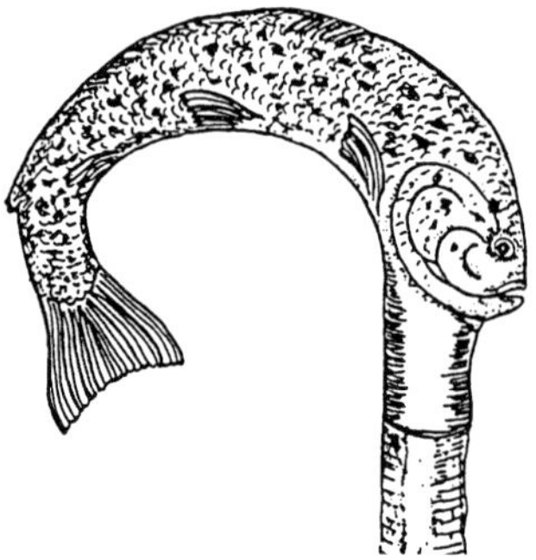

Antler Handles

Antler cannot be bent in the same way as ram's horn. Red deer antler has a honeycomb pith inside a hard shell, which in most cases needs to be reinforced, Depending on the type of joint required, method B or C. First I drill out the antler pith then check the hole size for method B in order to make a shouldered peg on top of the shank as it needs to be a firm fit. *(Refer to B. Fig. 22 page 30). (Method B or C are suitable joints).*

Sometimes I find it necessary to cap the crown or the tips of a handle in order to cover the exposed pith. *(Refer to Fig. 26 page 34).*

Whenever available I like to carve with stag antler of the Chital or Sambar Deer because they have little or no pith and being quite solid are ideal for carving with a rotary power tool fitted with a flexible shaft for ease of use. My power carver is ideal for intricate carving because I have a selection of high speed cutters to do the job how I would like it, on stags antler, horn or wood.

Sanding and polishing can be achieved with my power carver because it has a variable speed control that enables me to get the right speed for the job I'm doing.

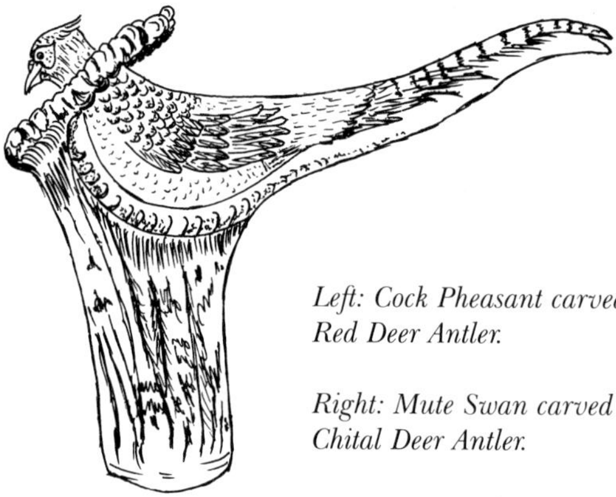

Left: Cock Pheasant carved in Red Deer Antler.

Right: Mute Swan carved in Chital Deer Antler.

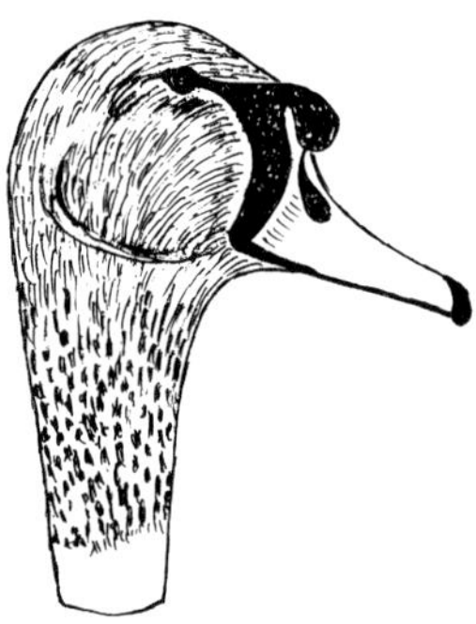

Chapter 7

ASSEMBLING

Jointing Methods

Joint A Fig 22
Jointing wooden handles, drill the handle first to accommodate a joint pin, which can be cut from 8mm studding about 135mm (5") long. This is a metal threaded rod normally used by Engineers. Mark the centre and drill an 8mm (5/16") hole into the handle neck 63mm (2½") deep, then glue in the pin. The 63mm (2½") protruding from the base is the joint to the shank.

In all cases the base of the handle should finish the same diameter as the shank top.

Joint B Fig 22
Ideal for jointing horn or antler and may be referred to as a peg joint because the top of the shank is shaped to form a shouldered peg 63-75 mm (2½"-3") long, and should be a push fit into the handle.

Joint C Fig 22
Using a threaded rod to joint antler is a little different, due to the amount of pith inside the antler shell the shell needs to be reinforced. Drill the handle neck, the finished hole size will depend on how much pith there is inside. A piece of wooden dowel should be fitted and glued inside the neck, when the glue is dry any excess wood should be cut off square to the handle base.

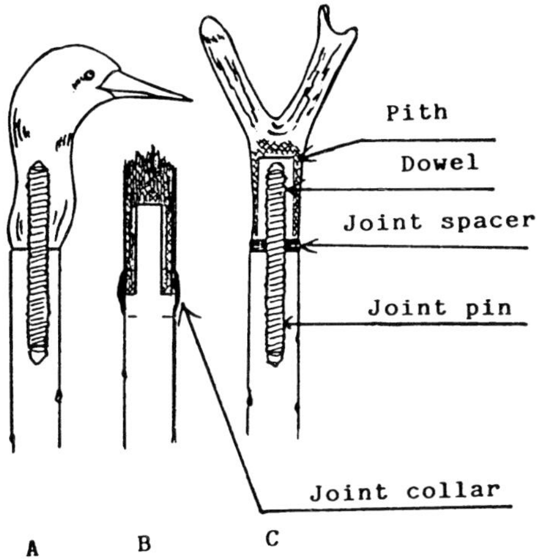

***Fig 22.** Jointing methods.*
A - Joint Pin using 8mm stud. B - Peg Joint. C - Joint for an Antler Handle.

Next drill an 8mm hole up the centre of the dowel and glue in a joint pin same as already mentioned in joint A *(Fig. 22)*. When fitting the handle to the shank using a joint pin you should drill a hole down the thicker end of the shank to suit the pin protruding from the handle base. Drill this slightly longer than the length of the protrusion, taking great care to ensure the hole is vertical in the shank. Before gluing the handle in place, have a dry run by trying the handle on the shank to make sure the joint is square. If not, it can be squared by sanding, using a sanding block in a rotary action. *(Fig. 23)*.

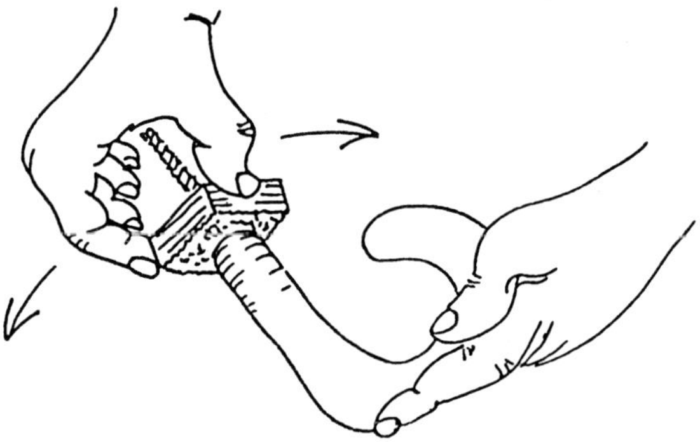

Fig 23 *Sanding block can be made from plywood. Glue a piece of abrasive paper to the base. When dry, drill a hole in the centre the same size as the joint pin.*

A similar method can be used to sand the top of the shank but a dummy pin Will have to be placed in the already drilled hole to act as a mandrel.

When shanking the handle to ensure that glue does not get onto the bark of the shank a piece of cling film may be wrapped around the top of the shank, making sure it does not go over the edge of the joint. Then make sure sufficient epoxy resin spreads on the joint pin and face joint, and a little down the hole in the shank. The excess glue will squeeze out of the joint as the handle is pushed into place, cramp in this position until the glue sets. When the glue is dry the handle or carved head can be tapered to finish the same size as the shank and any further carving or pyrography can be added at the neck area.

Dressing

Dressing the shank involves trimming off any unwanted twigs or the remainder of the thorns and cleaning these areas to a smooth finish. When the thorns from a Blackthorn shank have been removed the areas- need to be finished leaving the bumps standing proud, to give a knobbly shank. Any

holes or flaws can be filled with wood filler or emphasised with the pyrography tool. Finally rub the bark with 000 or 0000 steel wool, any dust can be removed by wiping with a fluffless cotton cloth, dampened with white spirit. For carved heads methylated spirits should be used. *(Also refer to Sanding Shanks on page 12).*

Cutting a Walking Stick to Length

The length of a walking stick is a personal matter and depends so much on a person's height and what feels comfortable for them. For myself I prefer a general purpose stick about hip height, a market stick to come just above my waist with a thumb stick or shepherds crook at chest height.

Making and Fitting Ferrules

These ferrules are fitted to the bottom of the shank. Horn and antler ferrules can easily be shaped on a rotary drum sander, but can also easily be made by hand by shaping with a file. In both cases a mandrel/handle will be required. Just drill a hole through a piece of antler to be a tight fit on the mandrel/handle to hold while shaping.

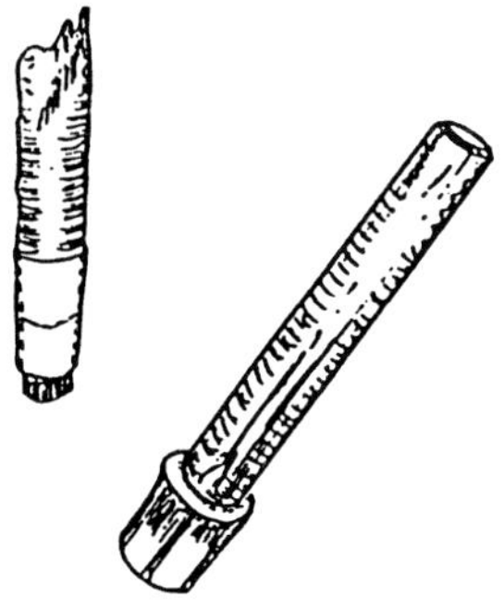

Fig 24 *R/H Mandrel with horn fitted to it for shaping a ferrule, L/H extended brass ferrule with rubber insert. This method can also be used to lengthen a stick.*

Ferrule forming is self-explanatory (Fig 25). First a tapered mandrel is required turned from round steel bar to match the bore of brass tube. Next cut square several pieces of tube to about the length of the mandrel taper. 1-2. knock the mandrel into the tube as far as it will go, 3. then tapping around the tube to release it from the mandrel 4. a ferrule is now formed, 5. shape the stick bottom and add a saw cut then secure ferrule with a wooden wedge.

I sometime make ferrules or collars in stag's antler while smaller pieces of antler will make ferrules but for collars just make sure the antler piece is large enough to go over the joint area of the stick. The pith needs drilling out and some filing will be required to make a perfect fit for collars.

Fitting antler ferrules, I normally only drill out the pith, and make a shouldered peg on the shank bottom to the ferrule length, the ferrule hole size needs to be a tight fit, then glue it on but it can be secured with a wooden wedge. *(Refer to B. Fig 22 and 5. Fig 25)*. Sometimes I turn horn or antler collars and ferrules on a lathe but the inside diameter needs to be drilled out first, the horn blank can then be turned on a wooden mandrel, abrading and polishing is also achieved in the lathe when in motion.

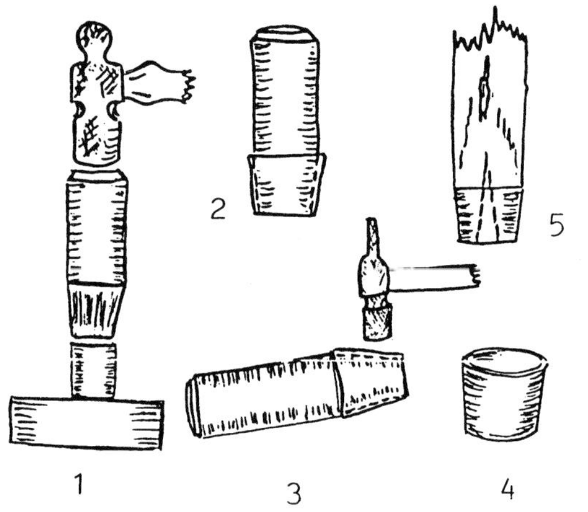

Fig 25. *Ferrule Forming.*

Not everyone wants to make collars or ferrules.
The illustration shows: Ferrules to protect the stick bottom. "A" British brass. "B" Horn. "C" Alpine spike for stony ground. "D" Rubber non-slip. "E" Joint Spacer mainly fitted for identification purposes. Joint Collars for added strength "F" Antler "G" horn. "H" Slipper mount to hide the pith on antler or decoration on stick handles.

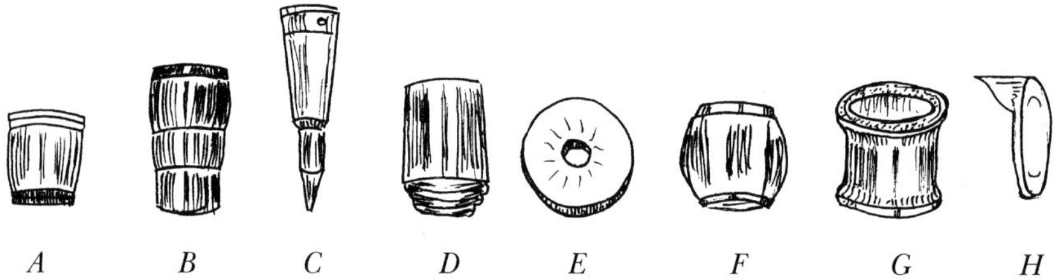

Chapter 8

MADE FROM ANTLER, HORN OR WOOD

Whistles

The tips from a stag's antler are best for making whistles because there is little or no pith inside.

First cut a piece of antler 63 to 89mm (2½" - 3½") long. Cut the tip off to leave the end flat to drill a hole down the middle, on a wooden whistle the end is already flat when cut to length. The depth of the hole will depend on the sound required, the deeper the hole, the lower the note will be. When the sound hole is cut, the angle of this can affect the tone of the whistle, the mouth piece can be shaped to suit the maker.

Now cut a piece of wooden dowel longer than required, to suit the already drilled hole, and file a flat on it approximately 2mm (5/64") and push it into the whistle so the end of the dowel is halfway between the sound hole, then try the note. If it does not whistle, push the dowel in further, or you may need to file the flat a little more to give a larger wind aperture. Trial and error will perfect the sound. Sometimes it may be necessary to seal the inside of a whistle this can be done by coating the inside with thinned-down P.V.A. adhesive. Set aside to dry before re-trying the dowel. When the whistle works to your satisfaction, the dowel can be glued in place and the unwanted dowel cut off when dry (refer to Fig.27).

Whistles can be built into walking stick handles. These are made in the same way, but if antler is used for the handle the crown may need to be sealed or a cap glued on.

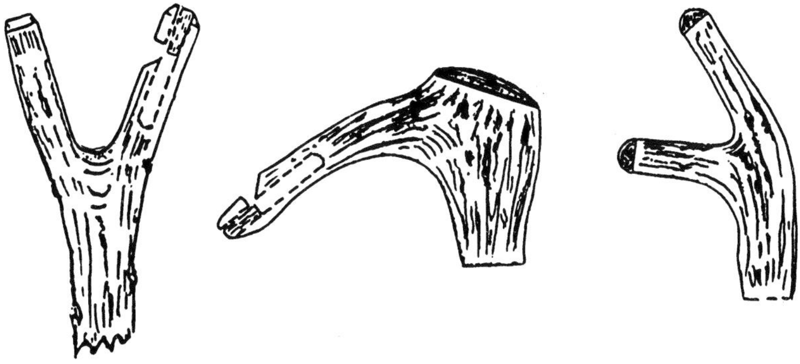

Fig 26 *Handles with built in whistles.*
Left: Wood thumb stick, Centre: Antler with the crown capped,
Right: As an alternative, cap the tips with horn or wood.

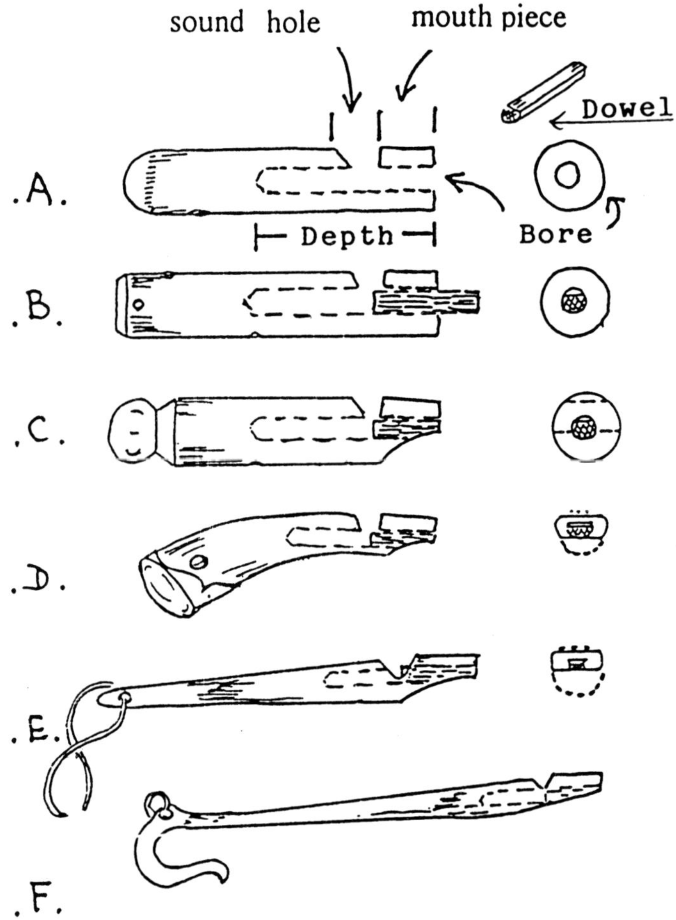

***Fig 27** Wood or Antler Whistles.*
'A' = Dimension, hole depth 45mm to 50mm. (1¾" to 2") x 6mm (¼") to 8mm (5/16") bore, slope sound hole from about 12mm (½"), mouthpiece 10mm (⅜") to 16mm, (⅝").
'B' = Pushing in the dowel to try the note.
'C' = Dowel trimmed off, mouth piece shaped.
'D' = A slipper mount can be glued on for decoration or to seal in the pith, always seal the hole wall intended for a thong
'E' = An antler whistle made this way should be fairly solid.
'F' = Rams Horn Whistles made from off cuts, dimensions for the bore, depth and sound hole may differ due to the size of material and the length depends on its design.

Buttons

Made from horn or antler. To make a set of four buttons 16mm (⅝") diameter, first cut four 16mm (5/8") dowelling by 100mm (4") long, to act as mandrels. Now cut four square pieces of antler for the button blanks, slightly larger than the intended finished size, by approx 6mm (¼") thick. Sand off behind the blanks to remove any pith, and make sure all four are of the same thickness. Now glue a blank onto each of the four mandrels. When dry, cut the corners off the blanks and file the buttons to shape just slightly proud of the mandrel, finish off with fine abrasive paper. Finally remove any sharp edges with a file. For the button holes, drill two by 2.5mm (3/32') holes through each button. Any buffing *(Refer to Page 28)*, can be done before removing from the mandrel, when cutting off the mandrel make sure not to cut the button. Finish the buttons by sanding the backs to remove traces of the dowel or glue, and dress the back edge, a twizzle with a small drill in each button hole will clean them up. The buttons are now ready to be sewn onto a garment.

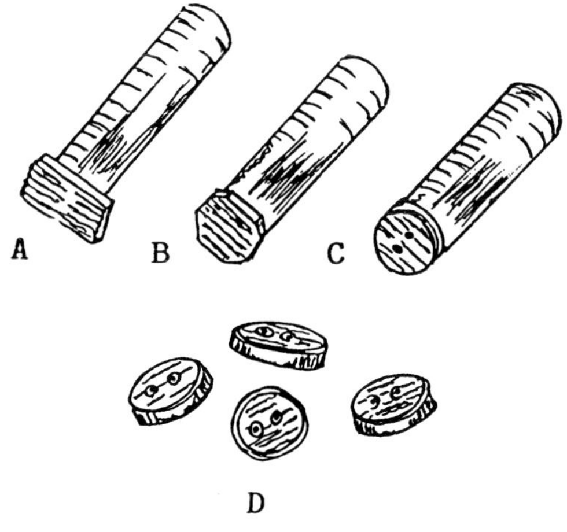

Fig 28 *Horn or Antler Buttons.*
'A' = Button blank glued to a mandrel,
'B' = Trim off the corners,
'C' = Shape with a file,
'D" = Finished buttons.

Making a Shoe Horn From Ewe Horn or Cow Horn

For making shoe horns a suitable jig is required. This can be made from a turned piece of wood 250mm (10") long and tapered from 48mm to 25mm (1⅞" - 1") . This forms the inside shape of the shoe horn. Also required is an outer forming plate, to make this bend a piece of thin sheet metal over the already made wooden former, and two jubilee clips large enough to fit over the jig. *(Refer to Fig. 29)*.

Prepare a piece of ewe horn by cutting it down the middle and cut off at approximately 130mm (5") long, leaving two halves. Boil a piece of the horn until supple enough to be flattened in between two plates in the vice and leave until set. The flattened horn will need to be sanded to a flat surface both sides. When the shoe horn blank is ready to be formed the size needs to be approx 38 to 50mm (1½"- 2") wide and no more than 3mm (⅛") thick.

Reheat the shoe horn blank until supple, place between the inner and outer jig and slide the jubilee clips on and tighten up. Leave the horn in the jig until set. When removing the shoe horn from the jig it may flex a little but this does not matter because this has been allowed with the diameter of the jig.

Next mark a centre line down the formed horn and mark the tapered sides to give approximately 10mm (⅜") radius at the top and 19mm (¾") radius at the bottom. Cut off the waste horn, smooth the edges, and polish the front and back. A hole can be drilled at the top of the horn to fit a leather thong.

Cow horn is ideally suited for making shoe horns because it is already partly shaped so the jig will not be required. First cut the horn down the middle giving two halves, choose the half with the most suitable shape, trim off a radius at the bottom and dress the edges. If a finger pull is required, heat about 38mm (1½") with a hot air gun and shape bend a curl over a piece of 16mm (⅝") dowelling. Finishing methods are the same as for horn handles. *(Refer to pages 27 and 28).*

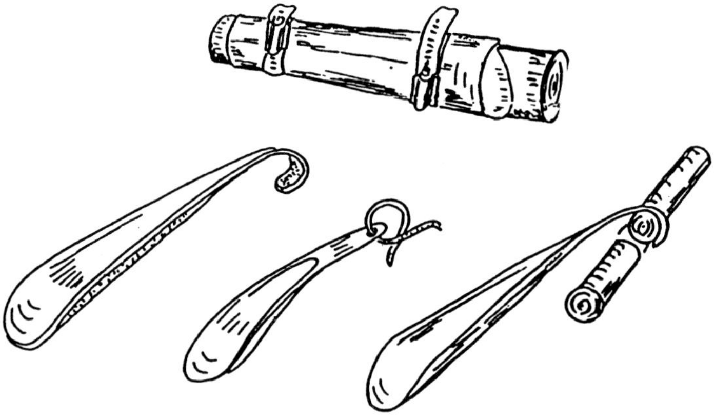

Fig 29 *Shoe Horn Jigs.*
Top: Ewe Horn Former.
Bottom Right: A finger pull can be formed on any shoe horn.
Bottom Left: Finished Shoe Horns

Chapter 9

COLOURING

The choice of brushes is very important, I like to have a wide range and ensure that they are compatible with the type of material being used. It is important to never let the colour dry out on a brush.

Palettes

Most colours can be mixed on a palette, however acrylic colours can be mixed on a plastic tray. A stay-wet palette tray is most useful for acrylic colours as they can be mixed and left on the tray overnight without drying out. For art material contact your local art supplier, always ask for leaflets and learn as much as you can before you make a purchase.

Colours

For many years I have used oils, the colours blend easily and dry slowly. This gives the carver/artist more time to get the colour correct before applying to the carved head. I also like acrylic colours, - these are water soluble and are easily blended. They dry quickly to a flexible surface and can be over-coated and over-glazed many times until the final finish is achieved. Beware of applying colours too thickly as they can clog up a textured surface, applying several coats of a thinner solution gives greater control over the final density of the colour. Acrylic colours when mixed with specially formulated mediums gives a wide variety of colour effects, and many colours can be created by mixing.

Prior to colouring, the bare wood will need to be sealed with acrylic "gesso". This is a white primer and can be overpainted with acrylic colour or oil paints. As an alternative cellulose based finish or thinned matt varnish will also seal the bare wood.

Starting to Colour

In reality birds structural colours are often due to particular light angles giving iridescent colours which constantly change. However, the non-iridescent colours do not change with the angle of view.

Colours and colour tones will vary depending on how they are diluted, what medium and how much is mixed, also between manufacturers so trial and error in blending is necessary.

When colouring a bird's head with a black plumage which also shows iridescent colours, it will be necessary to colour to a black glossed finish, and the colour sheens reflect through. This can be achieved with white over the already prepared sealed head. When dry apply base colours. These are then reflected by the white through the many wash coats of black. Normally wait for the first coat to dry before applying a second one, however, colours can be blended on a carved head whilst still wet, especially when one colour abuts the other or a colour tone is required.

The following notes on some species may help get you started:
Mallard (Anas Platyrhynchos) Male.

Eye 8mm dark brown, head dark green. Apply dark green to the head and blend if necessary, then overpaint a few wash coats of black. Bill - yellowish. *(Refer Fig 4).*

Scaup (Aythya Marila) Male.

Eye pale yellow size 8mm. Head black green - glossed.
Bill - Grey; Duck like. *(Refer Fig. 8).*

Gannet (Sula Bassanus).

The eye is sulphur yellow 6mm in size, predominantly white with buff suffusion of the head. The naked orbits of the face and throat are black. The ring around the eye is blue and the bill light greyish. *(Refer Fig 31).*

Great Northern Diver (Gavia Immer)

Eye is red, 7mm in size, head is black glossed with a green reflection. Incomplete neck bands are white, bill blackish eyelids tinted with brown, base colour used, hooker green. *(Refer Fig 31).*

Badger (Meles meles)

Eye colour used black, size 6mm. The badger is fairly straight forward as only black and white are used. Highlighting the hair with white to which a little silver may be added. Finish the nose in dark grey. *(Refer Fig 30).*

Moorhen (Gallinula Chloropus)

Eye blood red 6mm. Black plumage, red forehead extending to bill. Tip of bill yellow. *(Refer Fig. 8).*

Natural Finished Heads with a Hint of Colour

Natural smooth finished, carved or pyro textured heads (see also chapter on Pyrography).

American Wigeon (Mareca Americana)
(Part Texture) Eye 8mm Female, Middle Brown (Male same) Bill colour tone to blue/grey. (Refer Fig. 8).

Mallard Female.
Eye 8mm Middle Brown. (Texture) Burning creates the ducks colour when carved in a light coloured wood. *(Refer Fig. 4).*

Scaup Female.
Eye 8mm Lemon Yellow. Texture as Mallard with the addition of a white face blaze. Bill - Grey; Duck like. *(Refer Fig. 8).*

Goose (Family Anatidae)
(Part Texture) Eye Brown 7mm used (Male or Female) Bill - pyro shaded. *(Refer Fig. 8).*

Pheasant (Phasianidae Family)

(Part Texture) Eye 8mm Brown (Female). 9mm Sandy Yellow (Male) Bill - pyro shaded. *(Refer Fig. 30).*

Ring Neck Duck (Aythya Donavan)

Natural smooth finish. Eye 9mm Straw (Male). *(Refer Fig. 30).*

Lurcher Dog (X Breed) (Running Dog)

Eye, Dark Brown 6mm used. Smooth finish or hair texture by carving. *(Refer Fig. 8).*

The eye sizes I have used, other than actual sizes, relate to my designs in this book. Remember an eye when fitted will finish with a slightly smaller diameter.

Colouring with Drawing Inks

Drawing inks are water resistant and the various colours may be used over other coated colours when they are dry without fear of running. They may be mixed to produce varying colours and diluted with distilled water. The inks dry fast and have an excellent adhesion to horn.

Colouring a trout can be simplified by studying a real specimen. First apply colour washes to the body. When colouring start with a small area and study the body markings on both sides of the fish. When I have coloured the fish I leave the inks to dry for at least twenty four hours prior to adding a clear varnish finish. Drawing inks can be applied to wood but the wood will need a sealant coating first. Any handle that has been coloured with drawing inks, oil-based paints or acrylics when dry will need to be sealed by applying the appropriate varnish.

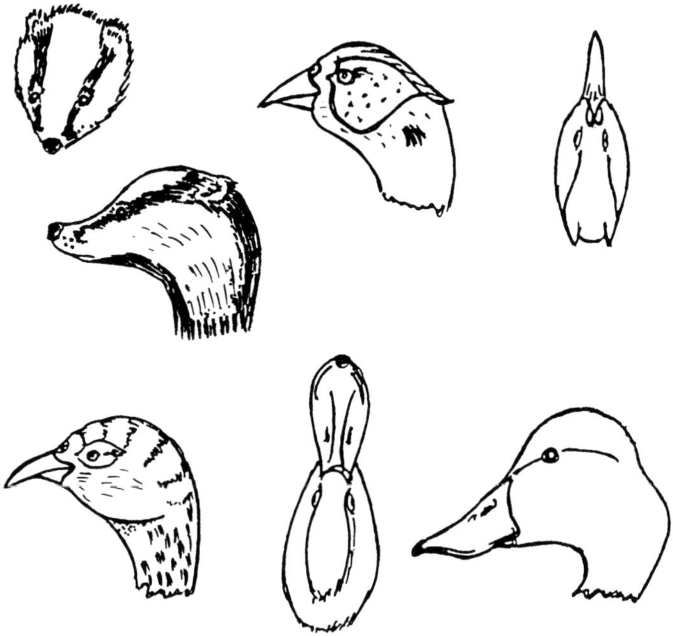

***Fig 30** Patterns ⅓rd Size, Top L to R: Badger, Cock Pheasant.*
Bottom L to R: Hen Pheasant, RingNeck Duck, Drake

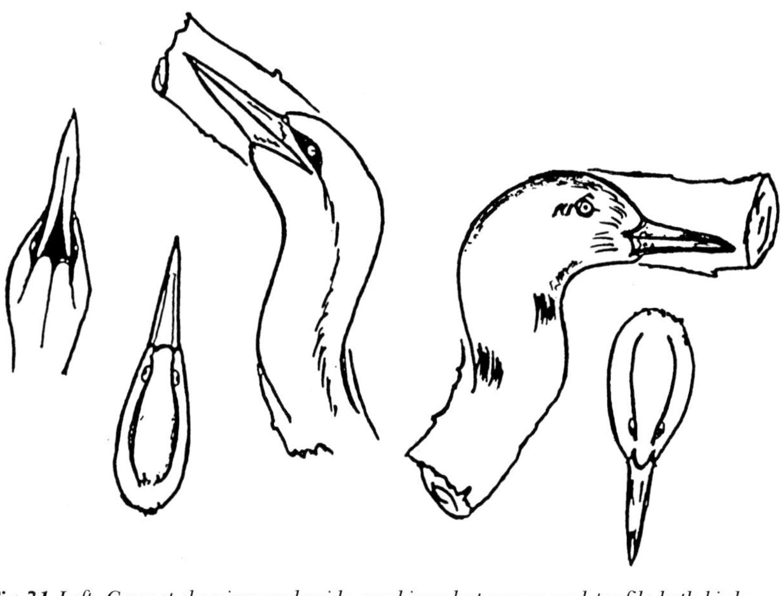

***Fig 31** Left, Gannet showing underside markings but crown and profile both birds.*
Right, Great Northern Diver, both in Twisty Ivy. ⅓rd Size.

Chapter 10

A RANGE OF FINISHING PRODUCTS

WOOD COLOURING

Colouring by fuming

Is a technique used to obtain various coloured effects on wood after the bark has been removed. Shanks are held in an airtight container in which an open vessel of ammonia has been placed.

Bichromate Stain

Made from bichromate of potash, also known as potassium bichromate. Bichromate comes in the form of deep orange crystals and is effective on any wood containing tannin. Initially deep orange, it quickly turns a deep brown. To make the mixture, dissolve 56 gms (2 oz.) of bichromate crystals in a pint of warmed water. When cool, bottle and dilute as required.

Van Dyke Crystals

Dissolve Van Dyke Crystals in warmed water. The quantity of crystals is varied according to the shade required. Strain through a piece of muslin to remove sediment. If one pint of stain is made then a tablespoon of 0.880 ammonia can be added to help the stain penetrate the wood.

Dyes for Wood

Commercially produced dyes can be mixed to produce various shades. Take care to mix dyes produced in the same range.

Staining Wax

Not really a durable finish for walking sticks but can alter the colour tone over a natural clear varnish. Can also be used to revive a well used stick.

FINAL FINISHES

Acrylic Varnish - Available in clear gloss or clear matt finish. If applied over any acrylic coloured head, leave for one week to harden.

Plastic Coating - This is a two part cold cure lacquer. It gives a durable finish on plain or painted wood. It dries to a flexible film and does not crack with movement. A good finish for wooden tops and shanks.

Yacht Varnish - It is well suited for walking stick handles and shanks. It gives an all weather long lasting durable finish.

Linseed Oil - Linseed Oil has been used by craftsmen for a very long time and is a natural protection for wood.

Tru-Oil - Gun Stock finish is the professional's choice for gunstock finishing also most suitable for walking stick shanks. It's a unique blend of linseed and natural oils, dries fast and will not crack with age.

Danish Oil - The ingredients used to manufacture Danish Oil penetrate deep into the wood and it dries to produce a low lustre durable finish.

Polyurethane - Is available in a clear gloss satin or matt finish and is suitable if you require a hard, durable finish. Useful for coating over coloured heads and for finishing over coloured horn handles. The matt finish is ideal to use as a wood sealant but needs diluting.

Cellulose Based Finishes - Can be applied directly to the wood in order to give a water and heat resistant finish. Can also be used as a sealant for the grain of wood.

Sanding Sealer is shellac based, used to seal the wood grain prior to applying french polish or acrylic colour on carved handles.

SUNDRIES

Wood Stopping - Natural or coloured, can be further coloured if required and will also take pyrography.

Wax Filler Stick (Beaumontage) - A small amount can be softened between the fingers and applied with a palette knife.

Shellac Filler Stick (Beaumontage) - This needs to be applied in a molten state and can be used for small holes and cracks.

Epoxy Putty - It is a two part putty, has many uses e.g. can be used when setting glass eyes in carved heads.

Paraffin Wax - Useful for sealing end grain during the seasoning of shanks or carving billets.

Bleach for Wood - Makes natural wood lighter and also removes weather stains.

White Spirit - is a turpentine substitute which may be used for thinning paints, varnish and certain wood stains. Also cleaning wood after sanding.

Methylated Spirits - Useful for cleaning horn, antler and wood carvings before colouring.

Ammonia - Strong ammonia may be used for wood fuming. N.B. .880 ammonia can be used in certain water stains, ask for "point eight eighty" ammonia.

Distilled Water - Can be used with certain colours to dilute them e.g water based inks.

Water Stains - When applied to wood raises the grain, to prevent this first dampen the wood with clear water to raise the grain, when dry rub down with abrasive paper, then apply the water stain.

When working with chemicals always wear rubber gloves and eye protection.

Chapter 11

STICKMAKERS MATERIALS

THE HIGHLAND HORN COMPANY LTD

Produce an extensive catalogue for all stickmaking materials and tools: include Water Buffalo horn, Red Deer Stag's Antler and pre shaped stick handles in wood or horn. A selective range of shanks in a variety of natural woods or Turned Ash & Hickory Shafts. Ferrules: Standard brass and Steel tipped brass, Sterling Silver or horn collars Buffalo horn forming plate ideal for forming Crook or market stick handles.

Taigh na Corrach, Knockmuir Brae, Avoch, Easter Ross, IV9 8RD
Tel: 01381 622488 Fax 0845 280 2225
E Mail highland.horn@btinternet.com

D.D. STICKMAKER

Telephone orders are most welcomed – evenings if possible please.
Tel: 01974 298566. Mail order list available.
Handcrafted Shepherd's Crooks & Walking Sticks. Supplier of Stickmaking Components include: Steel construction Horn Bending Jigs. Horn of Ram's, Buffalo and Stag horn, Wooden cut out blanks ready to carve. Preformed Horn Handles ready for finishing. Plan Sheets of full sized handles.

Mr. D. W. Davies, FRON–VILLA, LLANDDEWI BREFI, TREGARON, CEREDIGION, MID WALES, SY25 6RS.

THE KRAFTKABIN

For woodworking machines, tools, books and a range of finishing products and walking stick components.

248-254 London Road, Stoke on Trent, Staffs ST4 5RH
Tel: (01782) 416102 Fax (01782) 74[illegible]

PINTAIL DECOY SUPPL[illegible]

Materials f[illegible] ols, books, carving apparatus, art m[illegible]

20 Sh[illegible] , Cheshire CW5 SDF
Tel: (0[illegible]

RUSTINS LIM[illegible]

A wide ra[illegible] suitable for finishing wooden tops and w[illegible] types.

Waterloo [illegible] [illegible]ewood, London NW2 7TX
Tel: 020 84[illegible]0 4666 Fax 020 8452 2008

DENMAR SUPPLIES

Everything for a person who makes walking sticks. i.e. horn, antler, cut-out wooden blanks, shanks and components. Also country wear.

Walford Lodge, Walford, Baschurch, Shrewsbury SY4 2HL
Tel: 01939 260471 (Evenings after 4.00 pm)